HAL LEONARD BASS TAB METHOD

Written by Chris Kringel
Contributing Editors: Jeff Schroedl, Jim Schustedt, and Eric Wills

To access audio visit:
www.halleonard.com/mylibrary

Enter Code
2363-6525-3196-1620

ISBN 978-1-4803-7020-3

HAL•LEONARD®
CORPORATION

7777 W. BLUEMOUND RD. P.O. BOX 13819 MILWAUKEE, WI 53213

Visit Hal Leonard Online at
www.halleonard.com

MOVIN' UP THE FRETBOARD

In Book One, we learned all of the notes within the first five frets. Now let's move beyond the first five frets and start playing "up the neck." Here are the notes within frets 5–12 on the two lowest strings.

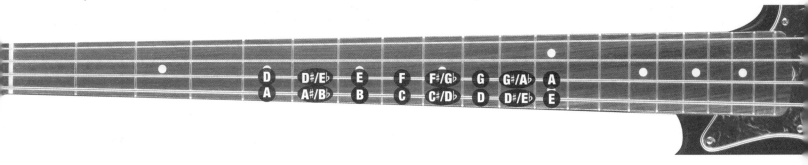

The following song examples utilize the notes on the E and A strings above the 5th fret. After becoming comfortable playing each riff, try naming the notes aloud.

GET READY

This song, originally written for the Temptations by Smokey Robinson, became a hit for the rock band Rare Earth in 1970. The riff is played up the neck at the 8th and 10th frets of the E and A strings. Starting with your third finger on the 10th fret will put your hand in the right position.

MY GIRL

Try this Motown classic by the Temptations. It's a perfect place to practice the rake technique from Book One. Remember? (i) = index and (m) = middle.

GOOD PEOPLE

Here's a bass line from Jack Johnson that jumps from the 7th fret up to the 11th fret. Try the fingering pattern written below for minimal hand movement.

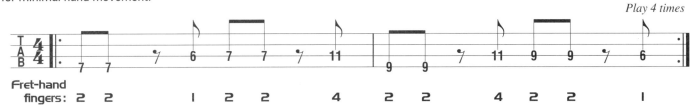

ONE LOVE 🔊

One advantage of playing on the lower two strings is that they have a bigger, beefier sound. In general, the larger the string, the deeper the tone produced. This song by Bob Marley and the Wailers could be played in first position, but then it wouldn't have the deep bass sound that is signature to the reggae style.

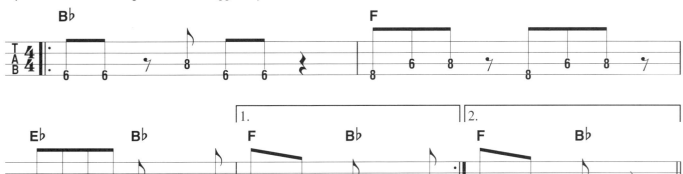

JAMMING 🔊

In this Bob Marley classic, bassist Aston "Family Man" Barrett lays down another great bass line using the low strings. This one can be played using one finger per fret, meaning each finger is assigned a fret. The 7th fret is played with the first finger, the 10th with the fourth finger, and the 9th is played with the third.

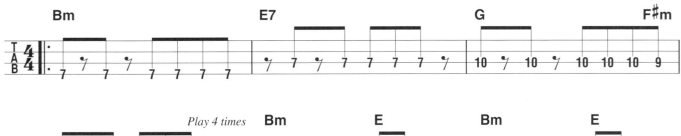

D STRING, FRETS 5-12

Let's add the D string in the mix. Here are the notes within frets 5–12 on the D string.

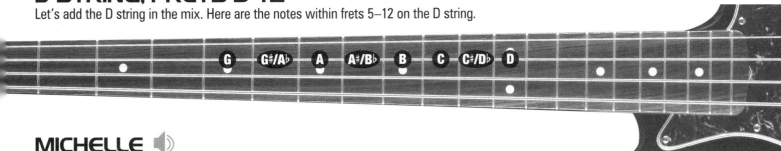

MICHELLE 🔊

Here we introduce the C and B-flat on the D string in this ballad by the Beatles.

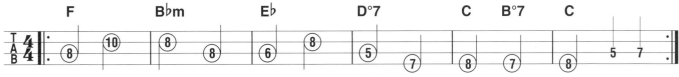

BEAST OF BURDEN 🔊

Here's a classic by the Rolling Stones that introduces the A and B notes on the D string. Remember from Book One that a staccato mark means hold the note shorter than its normal value.

staccato

I WISH 🔊

In this hit song by Stevie Wonder we'll tune down the open strings a **half step** (one fret). Some artists/bands tune down their instruments to accommodate a singer's vocal range or to sound heavier. In this case the E becomes Eb, A = Ab, D = Db, and G = Gb.

Tune down 1/2 step:
(low to high) Eb-Ab-Db-Gb

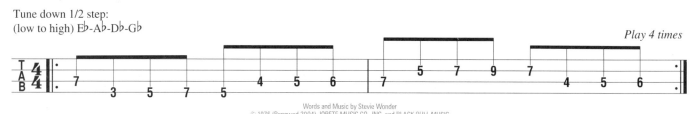

HOLIDAY IN CAMBODIA 🔊

This bass riff by the American hardcore punk band Dead Kennedys requires you to play two notes simultaneously, a technique called a **double stop**. Using a pick, strum with downstrokes across both strings so they ring out evenly in volume.

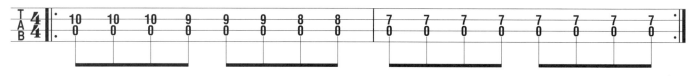

DRIVEN TO TEARS 🔊

For this Police song use the **box shape** that you learned in Book One starting at the 5th fret.

NOWHERE MAN 🔊

Here's another Beatles song from their album *Rubber Soul*. This one will be a challenge because of the syncopated rhythms at this faster tempo. Learn the bass part without the backing track at first, and once you know it well, try playing along. Begin each verse section with your 2nd finger on the 7th fret and stay in that position using one finger per fret.

Verse

1. He's a real nowhere man, sitting in his nowhere land,

making all his nowhere plans for nobody.

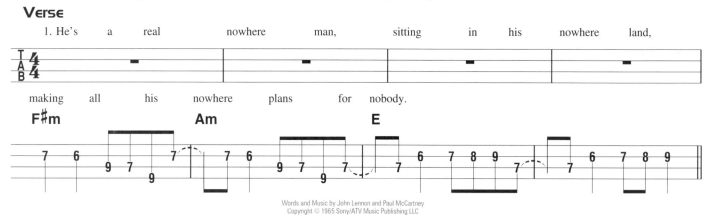

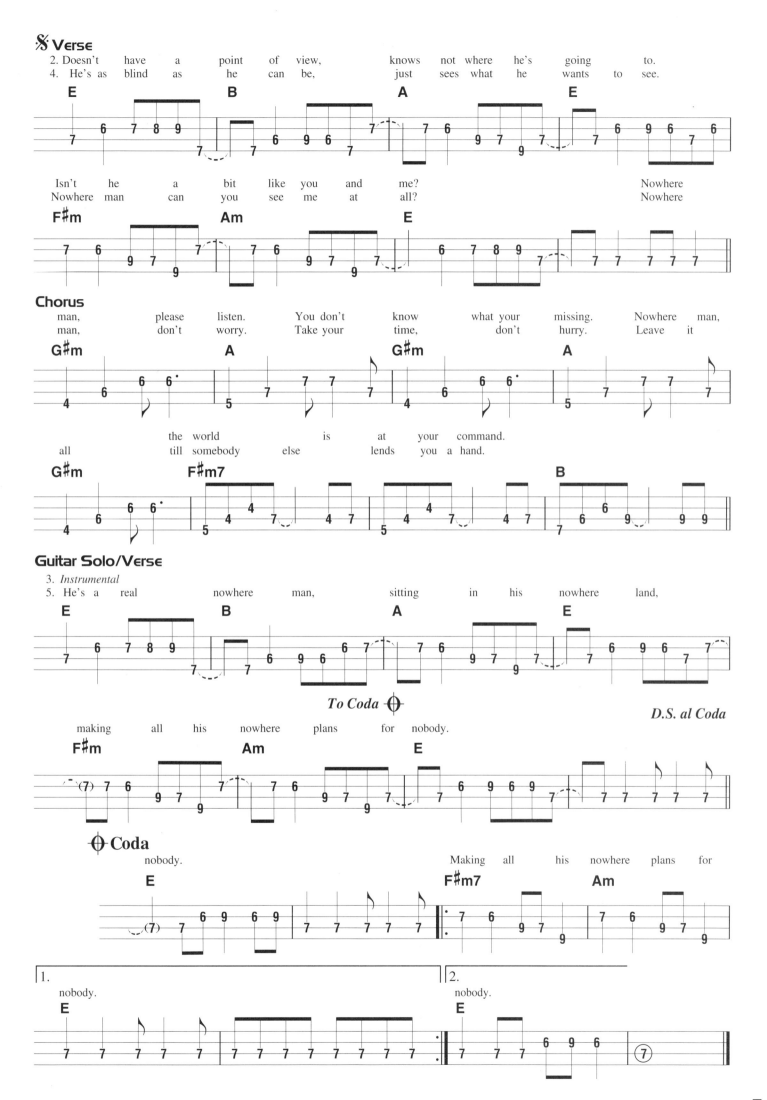

G STRING, FRETS 5-12

Here are the notes within frets 5–12 on the G string.

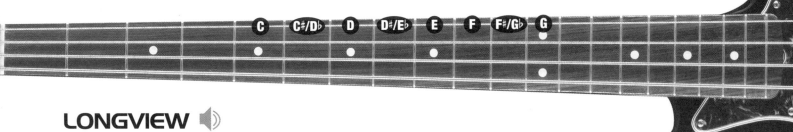

LONGVIEW

"Longview" is the debut single by the punk rock band Green Day. The last measure of this bass riff uses the G string, a hammer-on, and a double stop. Green Day tuned their guitars and bass down a half step to record the song, but for the purpose of this book, you can stay in standard tuning.

Play 4 times

Words by Billie Joe
Music by Green Day
© 1994 WB MUSIC CORP. and GREEN DAZE MUSIC
All Rights Administered by WB MUSIC CORP.
All Rights Reserved   Used by Permission

RUNAWAY BABY

Here we introduce the D-flat and E-flat on the G string in this song by Bruno Mars.

Words and Music by Bruno Mars, Ari Levine, Philip Lawrence and Christopher Steven Brown
© 2010 MARS FORCE MUSIC, TOY PLANE MUSIC, WB MUSIC CORP., MUSIC FAMAMANEM, ROC NATION MUSIC, NORTHSIDE INDEPENDENT MUSIC PUBLISHING, LLC, WESTSIDE INDEPENDENT MUSIC PUBLISHING, LLC, LATE 80'S MUSIC and ROUND HILL SONGS
All Rights for MARS FORCE MUSIC and TOY PLANE MUSIC Administered by BMG RIGHTS MANAGEMENT (US) LLC
All Rights for MUSIC FAMAMANEM and ROC NATION MUSIC Administered by WB MUSIC CORP.
All Rights for LATE 80'S MUSIC Administered by WESTSIDE INDEPENDENT MUSIC PUBLISHING, LLC
All Rights Reserved   Used by Permission

SUNSHINE OF YOUR LOVE

This song by the British rock band Cream uses a technique called a **bend**. String bending allows us to emulate the scooped notes of the human voice. The fret-hand fingers push or pull the string out of its normal alignment, stretching it so the pitch of the note is raised. For this song we will use a quarter-step bend which raises the pitch halfway between the note plucked and a half step (one fret).

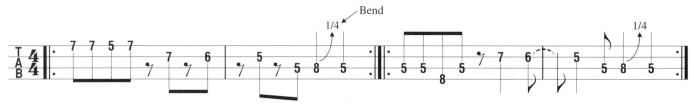

Words and Music by Eric Clapton, Jack Bruce and Pete Brown
Copyright © 1967, 1973 E.C. Music Ltd. and Dratleaf Music, Ltd.
Copyright Renewed
All Rights for Dratleaf Music, Ltd. Administered by Unichappell Music, Inc.
International Copyright Secured   All Rights Reserved

PERCUSSIVE

In this funky bass line you will notice an X in the tab staff instead of a number. An X represents a **muted note**. Muted notes (sometimes called dead notes) produce a percussive sound without an actual pitch that can be used to enhance the rhythmic feel of a bass line. For the example below, lightly lift your fret-hand finger off of the fretboard while still touching the string. Then strike the string with your picking hand to produce the muted sound.

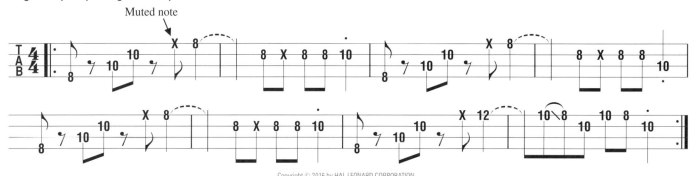

Copyright © 2016 by HAL LEONARD CORPORATION
International Copyright Secured   All Rights Reserved

DAY TRIPPER

You might remember this song from Book One. We simplified the bass riff at that time to help teach technique and reading, but the bass line here is the real deal. This is what Paul McCartney played on the Beatles recording.

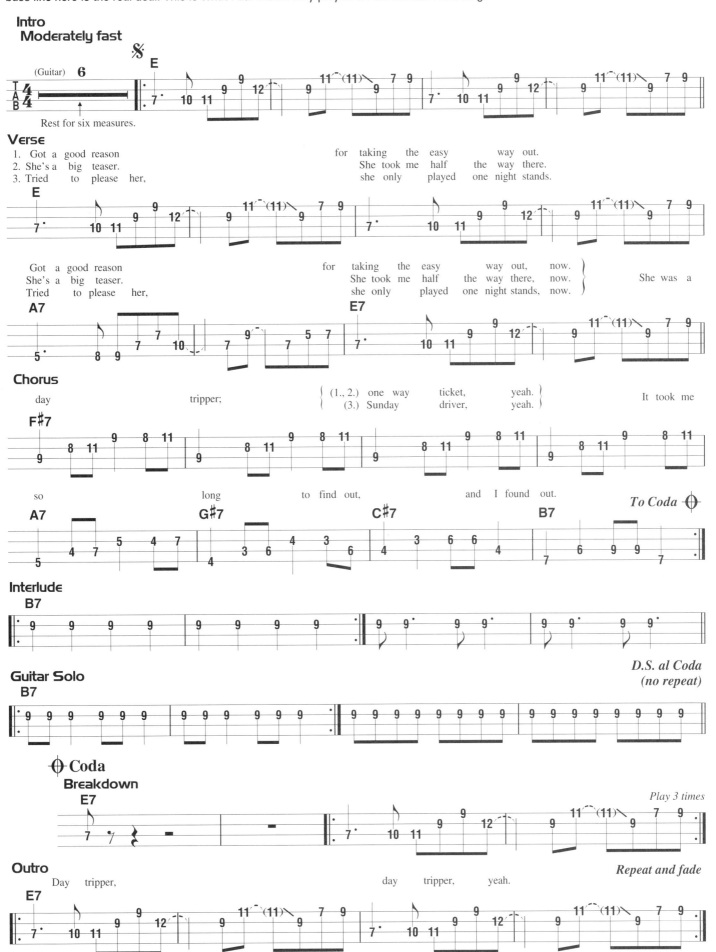

NEW RHYTHMS

A **sixteenth note** lasts half as long as an eighth note, and is written with two flags or two beams. There are four sixteenth notes in one beat.

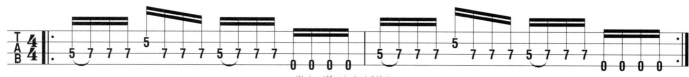

MOUNTAIN SONG 🔊

The main riff in this song by Jane's Addiction uses a repetitive pattern of sixteenth notes. Divide each beat into four parts, and count "one-e-and-a, two-e-and-a, three-e-and-a, four-e-and-a."

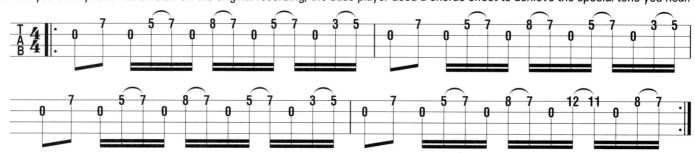

FORTY SIX & 2 🔊

Here's a fun intro bass riff by the band Tool. Be sure that all sixteenth notes are played evenly—the hammer-ons and pull-offs can throw you off if you're not careful. On the original recording, the bass player used a chorus effect to achieve the special tone you hear.

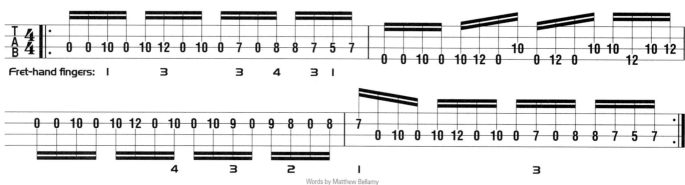

HYSTERIA 🔊

Ready to speed it up? With a pick, use steady, alternating downstrokes and upstrokes for the sixteenth notes in this song by the alternative rock band Muse. The movement of the notes can be tricky for your fretting hand, so there are a few fingering suggestions below the staff to help out.

UNDER PRESSURE 🔊

This highly recognizable song was from a collaboration between the band Queen and David Bowie. The second beat mixes an eighth note and two sixteenths.

WOULD?

One of the most popular songs by the band Alice in Chains combines eighth and sixteenth note variations on beats three and four. Count this one slowly at first to get the feel.

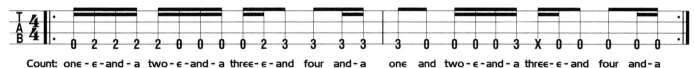

Count: one - e - and - a two - e - and - a three - e - and four and - a   one and two - e - and - a three - e - and four and - a

THE TROOPER

Let's continue on a theme with another great bass intro combining sixteenth and eighth notes, written by Steve Harris of the band Iron Maiden.

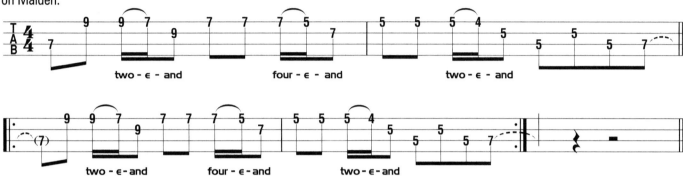

two - e - and   four - e - and   two - e - and

two - e - and   four - e - and   two - e - and

NO MORE TEARS

Clocking in at over seven minutes, this is the longest song recorded by British heavy metal vocalist Ozzy Osbourne. It starts with a double sixteenth-note pickup and introduces an **accent** (>), which tells the player to strike a note louder or with a harder attack than the surrounding, unaccented notes.

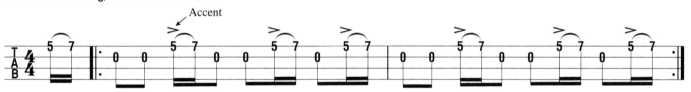

ACE OF SPADES

There's a sixteenth note tie in this classic metal anthem by Mötorhead. Go slow and count it through until the rhythm is familiar before playing.

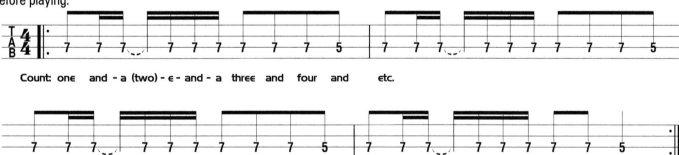

Count: one and - a (two) - e - and - a three and four and   etc.

GREEN STEW

This rock riff mixes groups of sixteenth notes with eighth rests. Descending bass lines similar to this one have been used in many songs like "25 or 6 to 4" by Chicago, "Brain Stew" by Green Day, and the end of "Stairway to Heaven" by Led Zeppelin.

A **sixteenth rest** takes up the same time as a sixteenth note, a quarter of a beat. It looks like this:

$$ \text{⅟} = 1/4 \text{ beat} \qquad \text{⅟} + \text{⅟} = \text{⅟} $$

SIXTEEN

To get started playing with sixteenth rests, try this rock groove at a slow tempo and count.

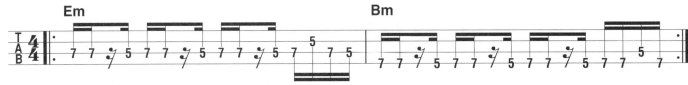

Count: one - ∈ - (and) - a   two - ∈ - (and) - a   three - ∈ - (and) - a   four - ∈ - and - a

FLY AWAY

This song was a hit for Lenny Kravitz in 1998. The part written here is the intro, and the funky, slap bass groove of the verses is taught later in this book.

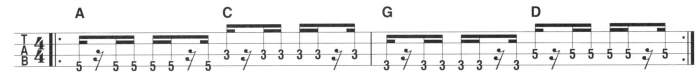

EXODUS

Here's a Bob Marley song for sixteenth note and rest practice.

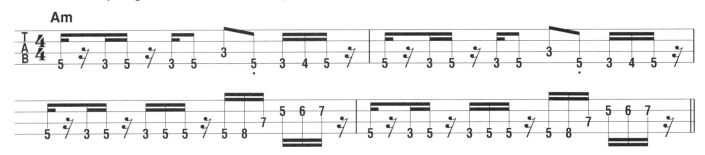

Another common rest pattern you'll notice when working with sixteenth notes is the **dotted eighth rest**. You've already learned that a dot after a note or rest increases the value by one half. Therefore, a dotted eighth rest lasts for 3/4 of a beat.

$$ \text{⅟} + \text{⅟} = \text{⅟.} \qquad \text{or} \qquad \text{⅟} + \text{⅟} + \text{⅟} = \text{⅟.} $$

SELF ESTEEM

This is a song by the American punk rock group the Offspring. On beat two, the dotted eighth rest takes up the last 3/4 of the beat and on beat three it takes up the first 3/4 of the beat.

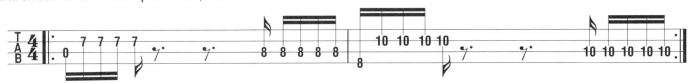

Count: one-∈-and-a two-(∈-and-a) (three-∈-and)-a four-∈-and-a   one - ∈ - and - a two-(∈ - and - a) (three - ∈ - and) - a four - ∈ - and - a

PLUSH

The Stone Temple Pilots recorded this song on their 1992 debut studio album *Core*.

Here's another common rhythm to learn and memorize—a dotted eighth and sixteenth note over one beat. It has two forms: a dotted eighth note followed by a sixteenth, and the reverse, a sixteenth note followed by a dotted eighth.

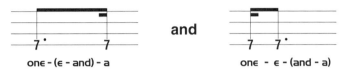

TWO WAYS OF ONE

First, try playing these rhythms with just one note to get the feel and to practice counting.

DANI CALIFORNIA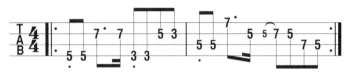

Here's an example of this new rhythm in a Red Hot Chili Peppers song. Also, notice the box shape (taught in Book One) within this bass line as it moves through the chord progression.

PEACE SELLS

The music video for this Megadeth song became an MTV regular and the opening bass riff was used as the MTV News intro. More recently, VH1 ranked "Peace Sells" at number 11 on their list of the "40 Greatest Metal Songs of All Time."

Play 4 times

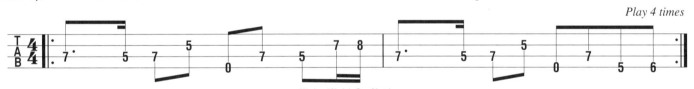

SWEET EMOTION

With this rockin' riff by Aerosmith, we introduce one more sixteenth/eighth note variation: a sixteenth–eighth–sixteenth pattern. Practice the new rhythm with just one note on the bass before attempting the song.

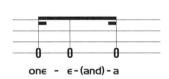

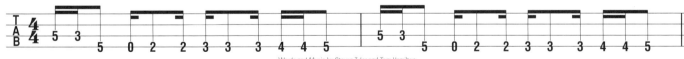

HARD TO HANDLE

Otis Redding wrote and recorded this song in 1968, and it later became the breakout single for the Black Crowes in 1990. Count aloud as you play through.

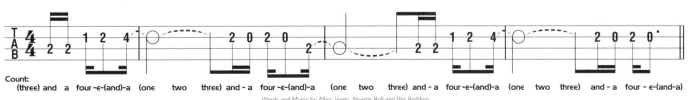

BRICK HOUSE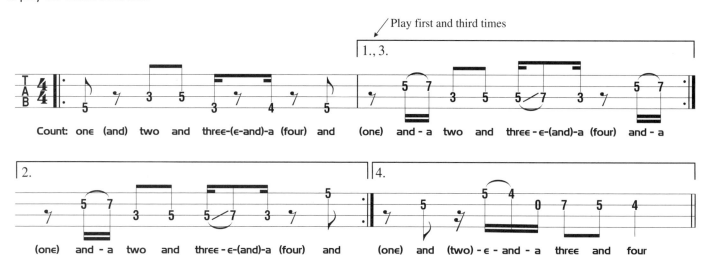

The various rhythms in this Commodores funk classic are a little tricky. Try learning each measure separately before attempting to play the whole bass line.

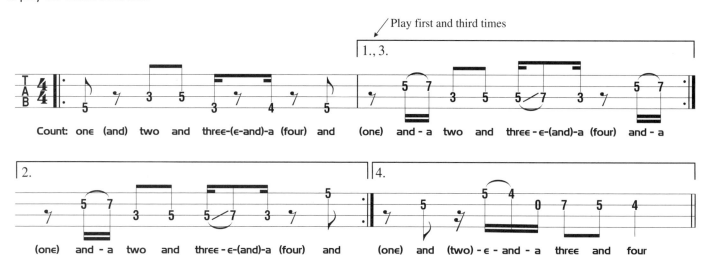

AMERICAN WOMAN

Now let's mix up the past few rhythms we've covered in this song by the Guess Who.

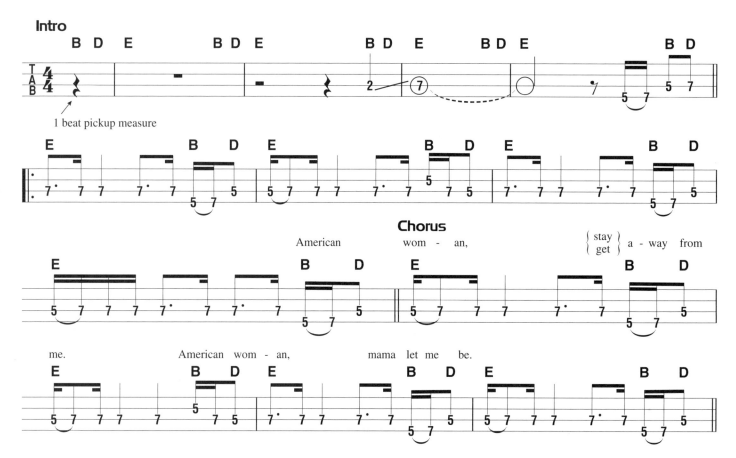

Verse

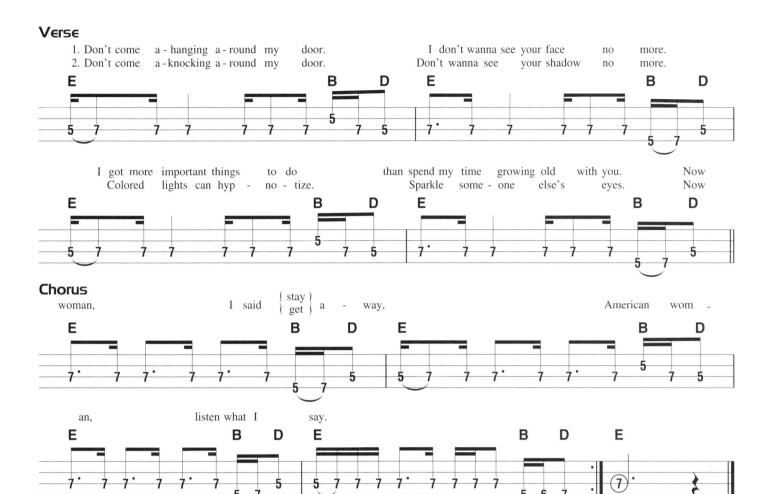

SHAKE YOUR BODY DOWN TO THE GROUND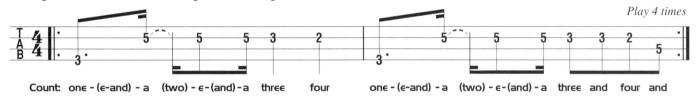

Counting becomes more of a challenge when adding ties to sixteenth notes, as is demonstrated with this Michael Jackson bass line.

Play 4 times

CAN'T STOP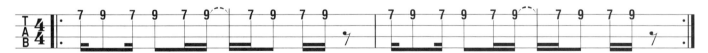

Here's the guitar intro to the Red Hot Chili Pepper's song "Can't Stop."

ROOT DOWN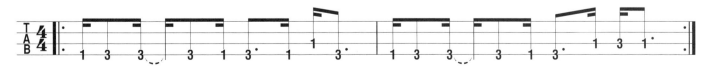

This funky, syncopated bass line was sampled by the Beastie Boys from a Jimmy Smith album and used as the main groove to their song "Root Down."

A **triplet** is a group of three notes played in the space of two. Whereas eighth notes divide a beat into two parts, **eighth-note triplets** divide a beat into three parts.

ADDAMS FAMILY THEME

While playing the riff from this classic TV series, count the new rhythm by simply saying the word "tri-pl-et."

Count: tri - pl - et   one   (two   three)   tri - pl - et   one   etc.

GET UP STAND UP

Here's another well-known Bob Marley song for triplet practice. Listen to the recorded example to hear what eighth-note triplets sound like at this slower tempo.

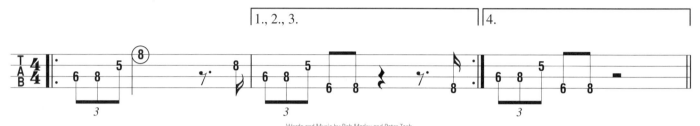

LONDON CALLING

Use your 1st finger to slide up to the 7th fret (E) from the 2nd (B). This will set up your hand in the correct position to reach the remaining notes. In the last measure, hold the C at the 8th fret for two beats before sliding down on beat 3.

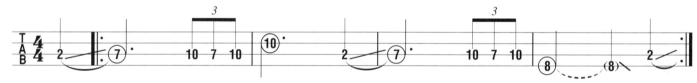

I'M YOUR HOOCHIE COOCHIE MAN

This is a blues standard written by Willie Dixon and first recorded by Muddy Waters in 1954. Count the beginning triplet figure with two rests the same way you've counted the previous triplets. A bracket above the notes takes the place of a beam to label the triplet grouping with rests.

Count: (tri - pl) - let   tri - pl - et

A **shuffle** is a bouncy, skipping, rhythmic feel. Eighth notes are played as long-short, rather than as equal values. This feel is the same as inserting a rest in the middle of a triplet or tying the first two eighth notes of a triplet.

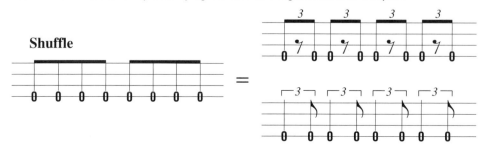

Shuffle

LA GRANGE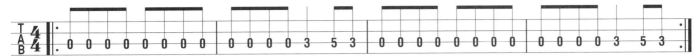

The shuffle feel is common in many blues and blues-rock songs like this one by ZZ Top.

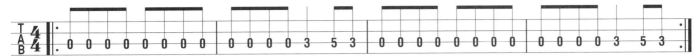

HIDE AWAY

First recorded in 1960 by Freddie King, this blues standard is a great example of the shuffle feel.

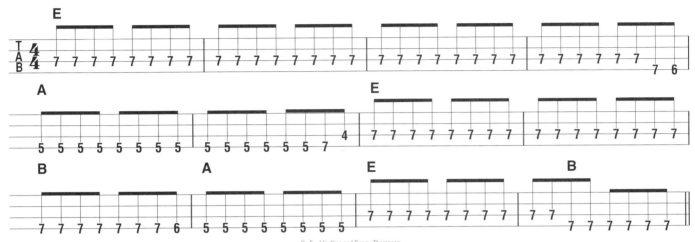

DETROIT ROCK CITY

Now let's speed things up a little with a vintage rock classic by Kiss.

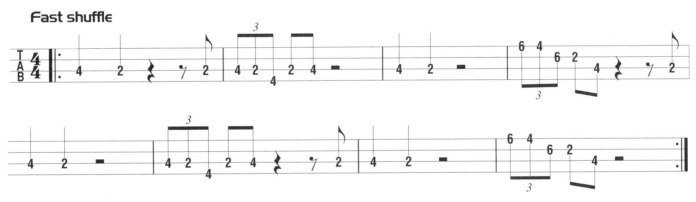

A **quarter-note triplet** divides two beats into three equal parts. For example, the three quarter notes in this triplet equal the same as two regular quarter notes.

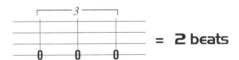

= 2 beats

HOLD THE LINE

Observe the counting below the tab of this riff by the band Toto.

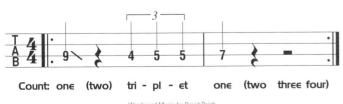

Count: one (two) tri - pl - et   one (two three four)

TRIPLET WALK

Before playing this next practice example, try tapping your foot with a steady, quarter-note pulse. Then, at the same time, say "tri-pl-et, tri-pl-et" with the quarter-note triplet rhythm. If you can do that, you've got it!

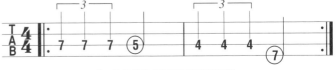

THE BOYS ARE BACK IN TOWN

Try playing this full song for more practice with triplets and the shuffle feel. On the original, classic recording by Thin Lizzy, the band tuned their instruments down a half step, but this recording is in standard tuning.

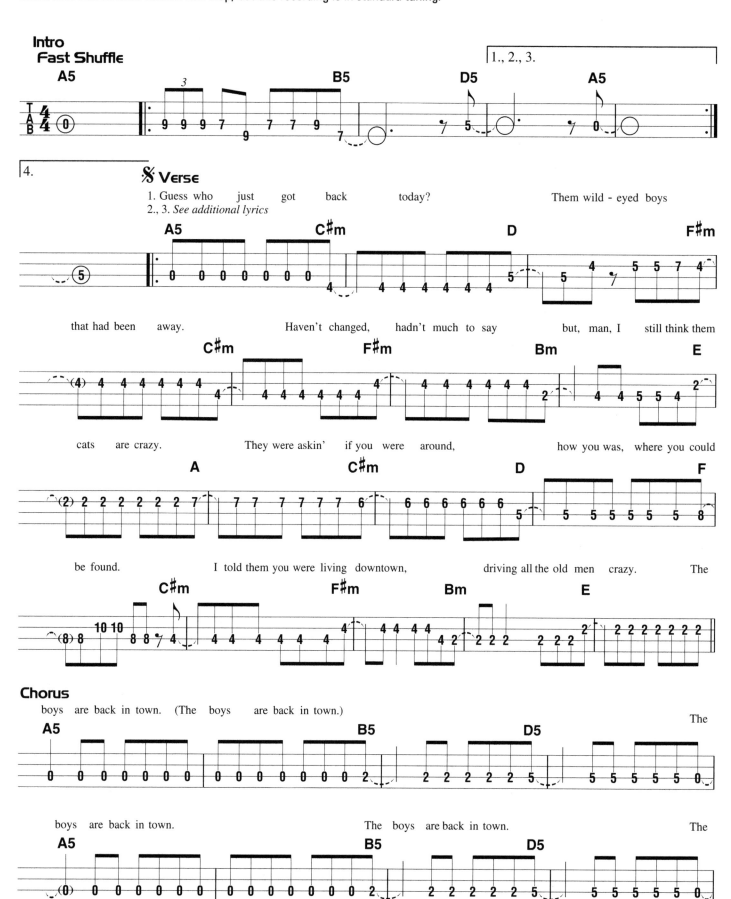

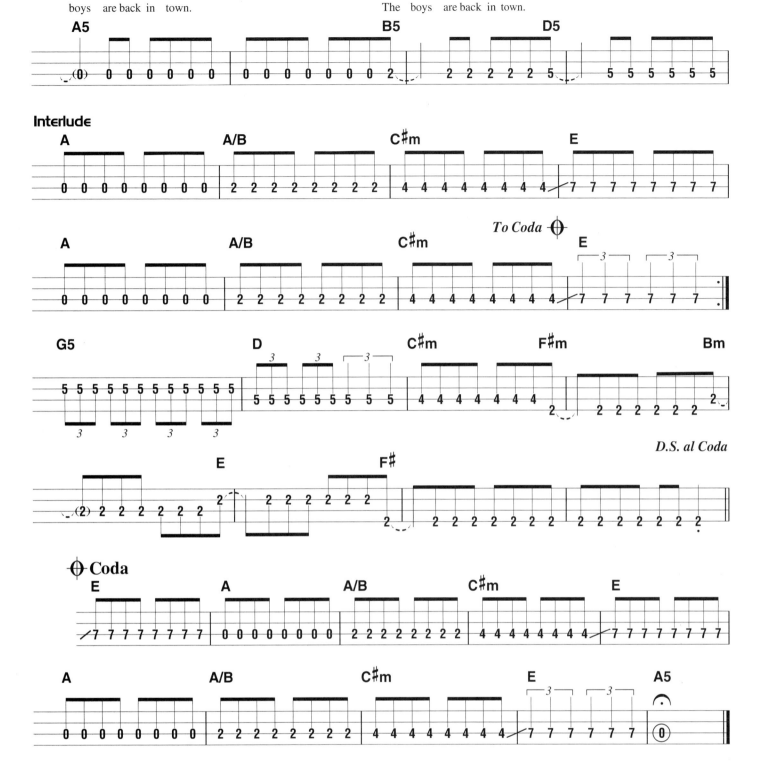

Additional Lyrics

2. You know that chick that used to dance a lot?
   Every night she'd be on the floor shakin' what she got.
   Man, when I tell you she was cool, she was red hot.
   I mean she was steamin'.
   And that time over at Johnny's place,
   Well, this chick got up and she slapped Johnny's face.
   Man, we just fell about the place.
   If that chick don't want to know, forget her.

3. Friday night they'll be dressed to kill
   Down at Dino's Bar and Grill.
   The drink will flow and blood will spill,
   And if the boys wanna fight, you better let 'em.
   That jukebox in the corner blasting out my favorite song.
   The nights are getting warmer, it won't be long.
   Won't be long till summer comes,
   Now that the boys are here again.

MOVIN' UP THE FRETBOARD: PART 2

Now that you've learned all of the notes within the first twelve frets, let's move on. Starting at fret 12, the entire note sequence repeats. In other words, fret 12 of the low E string has the same name as the open string (E), fret 13 has the same name as fret 1 (F), fret 14 is the same as fret 2, and so on. The notes above the 12th fret sound an octave above their lower counterparts. Let's take a look.

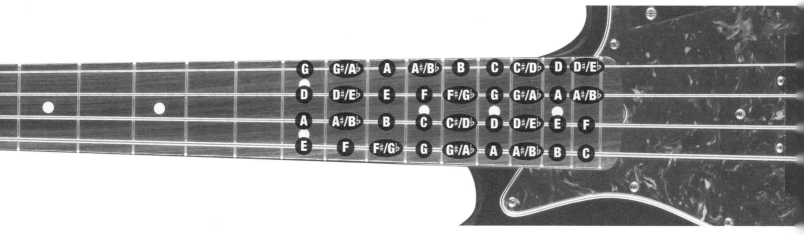

SWEET EMOTION

This bass intro from the band Aerosmith starts at the 12th fret of the A string. Begin with your 2nd finger and hold it there throughout the riff. Use your 3rd and 4th fingers for the G and A notes on the G string, respectively.

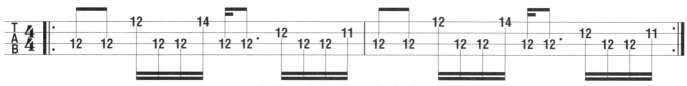

BY THE WAY

Here's another bass line by one of the most popular bassists in rock music, Flea of the Red Hot Chili Peppers. This one begins way up high on the neck. Once you reach the eighth measure you will see the instructions "D.C. al Fine," which means jump back to the beginning of the piece and end at the measure marked "Fine" (pronounced fee'-nay).

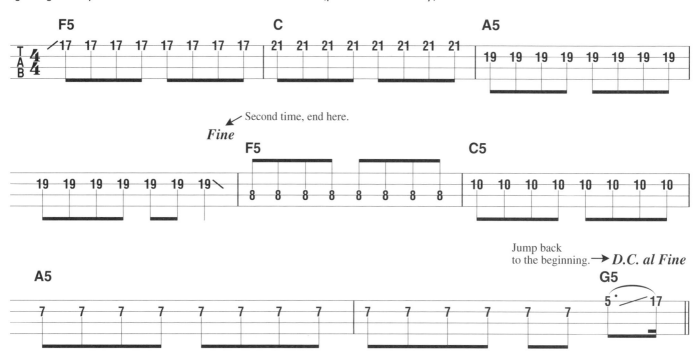

THE MAJOR SCALE

A **scale** is a group of notes ascending or descending in a specific order. In western music the most common scale is the **major scale**. It can be built starting on any root note, and follows a specific pattern of **whole steps** (2 frets) and **half steps** (one fret). The major scale includes one note each from the musical alphabet. Here it is beginning on the low E string.

E MAJOR SCALE

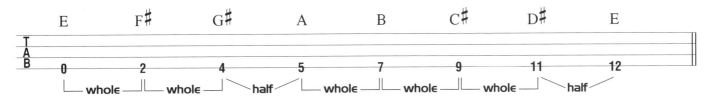

Although it's easy to visualize the scale pattern along one string, it's not always practical to play it this way. The bass neck is a grid which makes it easy to memorize patterns or shapes. Every scale can be learned as a movable pattern of notes, and you can move that pattern anywhere on the neck to play the scale in any key. Here is the standard fingering for playing the major scale on the bass.

G MAJOR SCALE

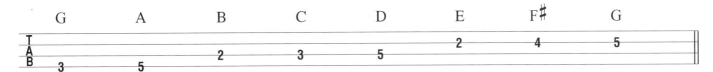

The scale above starts on the note G, so it's a G major scale. If you move the pattern to the A string and start on the note C it becomes a C major scale. If you move the pattern up two frets from C, it becomes a D major scale.

C MAJOR SCALE

D MAJOR SCALE

Practicing scales is a great way to develop fret-hand dexterity. Start slowly, and gradually build up speed.

Here's another way to visualize the major scale pattern. The root is another word for the starting note of the scale.

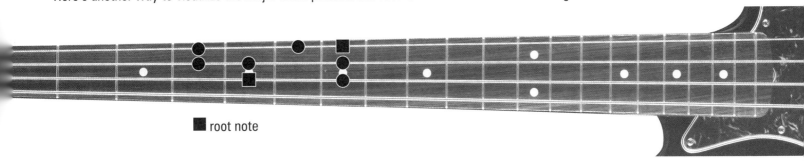

■ root note

The notes of the major scale are the foundation for countless melodies, bass lines, solos, and chord progressions. Here are some examples.

DO-RE-MI 🔊

This song from *The Sound of Music* is one of the most famous uses of the major scale in popular music. The lyrics teach the seven solfege syllables commonly used to sing the major scale. The melody mostly consists of notes from the C major scale, and shifts to D major and E major in measures 11 and 13, respectively.

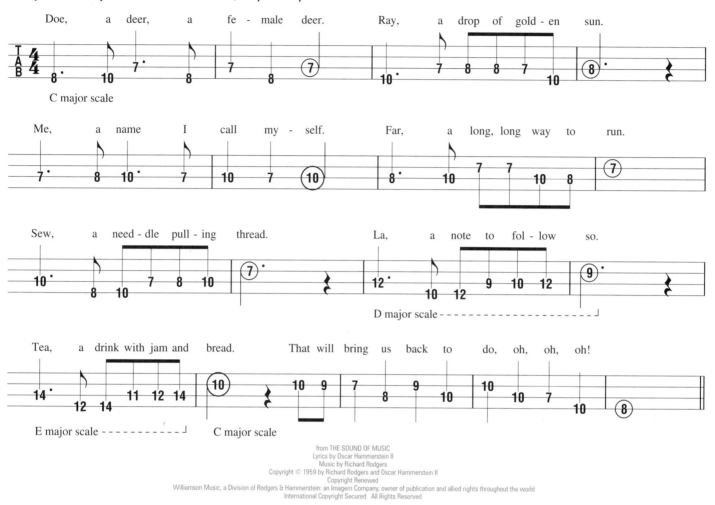

JOY TO THE WORLD 🔊

The melody of this famous Christmas carol, by Baroque composer George Frideric Handel, uses all of the notes in the D major scale.

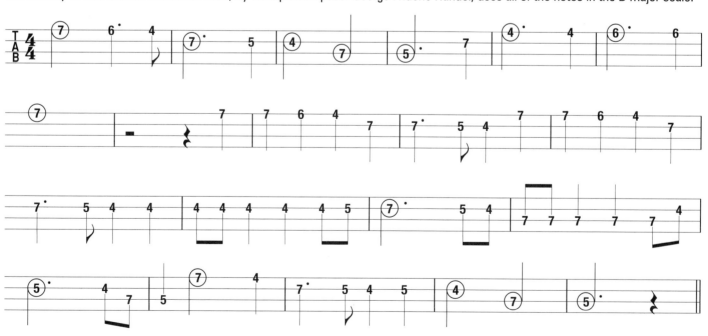

MUSIC THEORY 101

When the notes of a song come from a particular scale, we say that the song is in the key of that scale. For example, if the notes of a song all come from the D major scale, we say that the song is in the key of D major.

LEAN ON ME 🔊

The intro to "Lean on Me" by Bill Withers uses notes exclusively from the C major scale, therefore it is in the key of C.

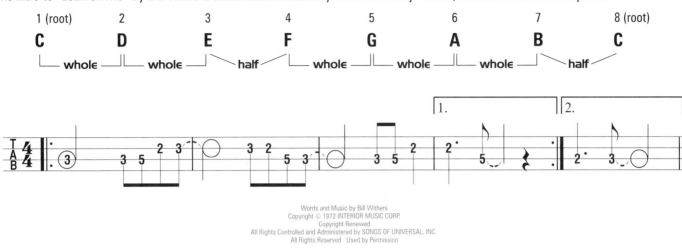

Words and Music by Bill Withers
Copyright © 1972 INTERIOR MUSIC CORP.
Copyright Renewed
All Rights Controlled and Administered by SONGS OF UNIVERSAL, INC.
All Rights Reserved   Used by Permission

Notice how the bass line sounds "at rest" when you arrive at the last note (C)? This is because the C note is the root, or **tonic**—the note around which the key revolves.

MAJOR SCALE CHART

Major scales are the building blocks of music and music theory. Chords, chord progressions, and bass lines are all derived from scales. Here is a handy table that spells the notes in all 12 keys. Don't get bogged down trying to memorize it all at once, but you might want to dog-ear this page for future reference.

	1 (root)	**2**	**3**	**4**	**5**	**6**	**7**
C major	C	D	E	F	G	A	B
G major	G	A	B	C	D	E	F♯
D major	D	E	F♯	G	A	B	C♯
A major	A	B	C♯	D	E	F♯	G♯
E major	E	F♯	G♯	A	B	C♯	D♯
B major	B	C♯	D♯	E	F♯	G♯	A♯
F♯ major	F♯	G♯	A♯	B	C♯	D♯	E♯
D♭ major	D♭	E♭	F	G♭	A♭	B♭	C
A♭ major	A♭	B♭	C	D♭	E♭	F	G
E♭ major	E♭	F	G	A♭	B♭	C	D
B♭ major	B♭	C	D	E♭	F	G	A
F major	F	G	A	B♭	C	D	E

THE MINOR SCALE

Another common scale is the **natural minor scale**. Just like the major scale it can be built starting on any root note and follows a specific pattern of whole and half steps. Here it is beginning on E.

E MINOR SCALE

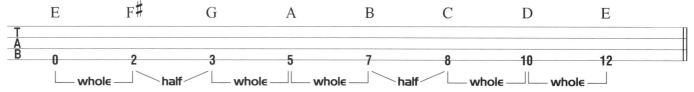

G MINOR SCALE

Here is the standard fingering and shape for playing a minor scale. We will start on the note G.

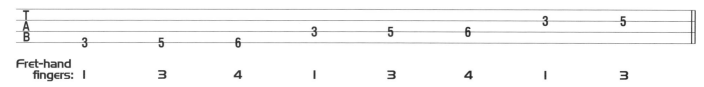

A MINOR SCALE/D MINOR SCALE

Now let's move it up two frets and start on A. After that, move up to the 3rd string and start on the root note D. The pattern remains the same when you move across these two strings.

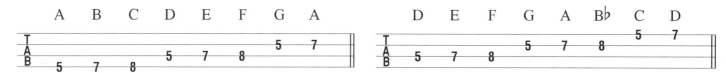

Here is another way to visualize the minor scale pattern.

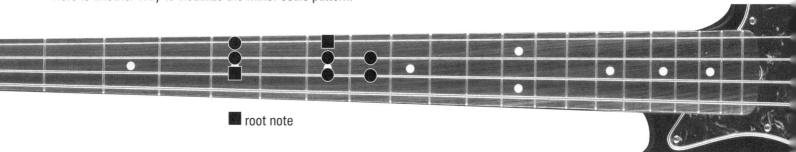

■ root note

ROCK LOBSTER

The C minor scale is in prominent use for the main riff of this fun and quirky B-52's song. Originally, this part was played on an electric guitar (tuned low), but it sounds great on bass too.

ROUNDABOUT

The E minor scale with the root on the open string retains the same pattern, except any note you would normally fret with the first finger is now an open string instead. Play this bass line by Chris Squire of Yes with a pick to execute the muted notes. Practice slowly!

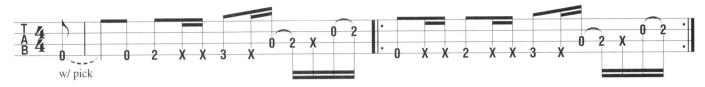

SMOOTH CRIMINAL

"Smooth Criminal" is from Michael Jackson's 1987 album *Bad*. The bass part uses four notes from the A minor scale: the root, 2nd, 3rd, and 7th. The 7th of the scale here (G) is played below the root note at the third fret, an octave below its place in the scale pattern.

DRIVE

Here is a song from R.E.M. The intro bass part is built from the D minor scale, which sounds great beneath the guitar's strummed D minor chord.

MAJOR AND MINOR TRIADS

A **triad** is a set of three notes from a scale—the root, 3rd, and 5th—that are used to form the basic **chords** a guitarist or pianist would play. While these instruments play the notes simultaneously for a chord, bassists play them separately and use the notes to create bass lines that support those chords.

All triads are labeled by their root note. The chord symbol "C" indicates a C major triad which is built from the root, 3rd, and 5th of the major scale.

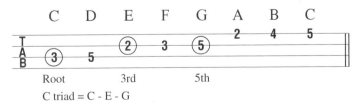

We can create a minor triad the same way by playing the root, 3rd, and 5th of the minor scale. Let's look at a C minor triad. All minor triads are labeled with the root and a lowercase "m" to indicate minor, for example: Cm.

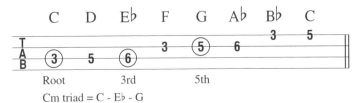

HOUND DOG

The bass line in this classic song made famous by Elvis Presley uses just a triad for each chord change until the tenth measure, where it walks down the F major scale to C.

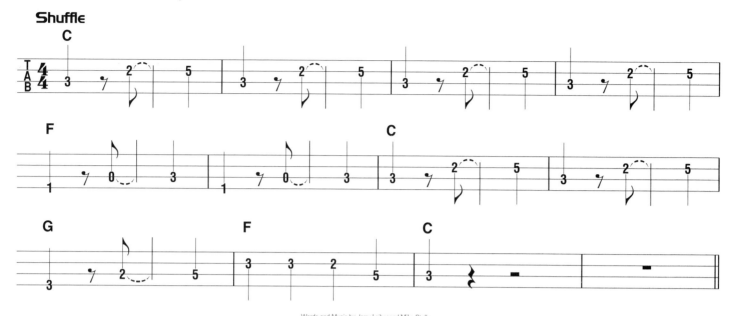

IN THE MIDNIGHT HOUR

In this song by Wilson Pickett, the bass line outlines a major triad for each E, A and B chord. Note the triad pattern starting on the open string for the E and A chords.

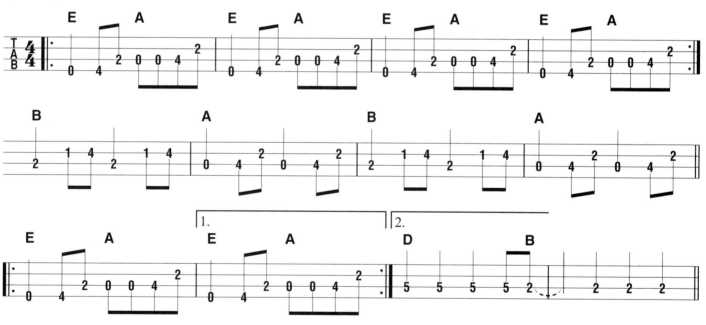

EIGHT DAYS A WEEK

"Eight Days a Week" is another great song by the Beatles. For the verse section, Paul McCartney outlines a triad over the G and E chords, but for the D he walks down using a root, 6th, 5th and 3rd from the D major scale.

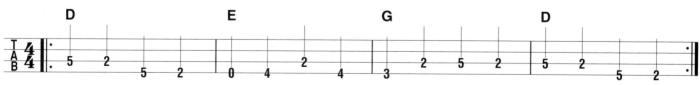

WHITE WEDDING

This classic Billy Idol song has a hypnotic bass line that centers on a B minor triad.

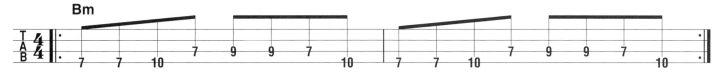

COME TOGETHER

"Come Together" is the first track on the Beatles album *Abbey Road*. Its distinctive opening riff consists of only notes from the D minor triad. Instead of playing the low D on the 10th fret of the E string where the rest of the riff is positioned, Paul plays it at the A string's 5th fret, and slides up to the next note for a unique musical effect. Use your 3rd finger to slide up.

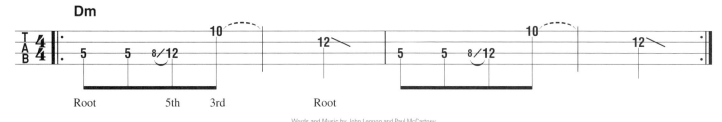

CREATING BASS LINES

Triads and scales are the building blocks of music, and knowing them is the key to creating bass lines. But how do you begin to use these tools to write your own bass parts?

START WITH THE ROOT

As bassists, our main job is to support the harmony (chords) of a song while also locking in with the rhythm. Sometimes all it takes to do the job right is to play the root notes of each changing chord. Some of the greatest songs have been played this way, including "With or Without You" by the band U2.

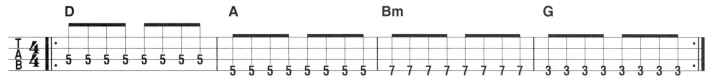

ADD THE FIVE

An absolute standard of bass lines is the root–5th pattern. Found in countless songs in all genres, this is a fool-proof way of creating a solid, functional line. Like the root-only approach above, this pattern moves to match each chord. Always place the root note on the first beat of each new chord.

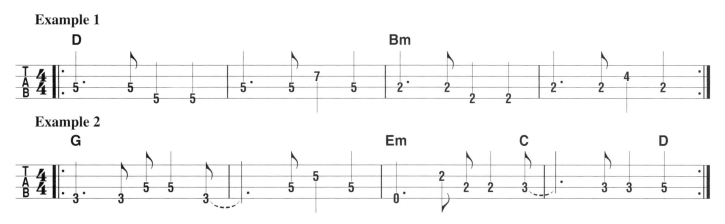

MIX IN A THIRD

Sometimes all a song needs is a root or root–5th line, and anything more would be superfluous. However, the addition of a third can create a different flavor. You may have noticed that the root–5th relationship stays the same regardless of whether the chord is major or minor. In contrast, we have to match the correct 3rd to the major or minor quality of the chord being played.

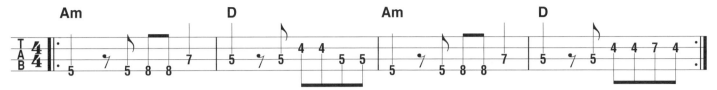

PASSING TONES

Up to this point, we've only used the notes of the triads to compose bass lines, and they are the most important notes we can use; they literally outline the chords other instruments are playing. We have more options, though, taking advantage of minor and major scales to find passing tones. These notes can help us bring a line smoothly from one chord to the next.

In "Orange Crush" by R.E.M., the F-sharp in the 2nd measure of the bass line acts as a passing tone from the Em chord to the G. Then in measure 3, the C acts as a passing tone from the 3rd of the G chord (B) to the root of the following D chord.

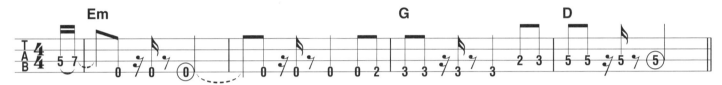

Using the concepts just described, try and create your own bass lines over the following chord progression.

JANGLY

Rhythm slashes like the ones in these measures tell the bass player they must improvise a part for the given chords. Play along with the audio backing track to experiment with creating your own bass lines.

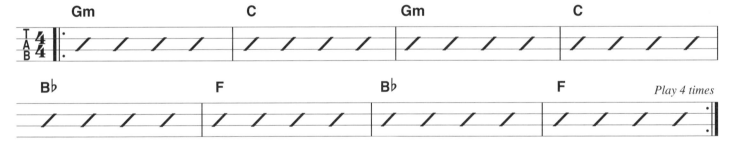

OTHER TIME SIGNATURES

All the song examples presented so far have been in the two most common meters: 4/4 and 3/4. These aren't the only time signatures in town, though. Let's explore a few more variations.

BLACK SUNSHINE

The "Black Sunshine" riff by White Zombie is in **6/4 time**. This means there are six beats in each measure, and a quarter note lasts one beat.

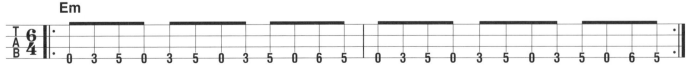

Count: one and two and three and four and five and six and

TAKE FIVE 🔊

This jazz favorite by Dave Brubeck is in **5/4 time**. For all time signatures, the top number of the fraction tells how many beats there are per measure, and the bottom number tells what kind of note equals one beat. So, one measure in this song has five quarter notes (five beats).

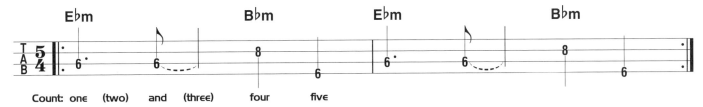

Count: one (two) and (three) four five

MONEY 🔊

"Money" is a song from the rock band Pink Floyd and is possibly the most recognizable riff in **7/4 time**. One measure in this tune has seven quarter notes (seven beats).

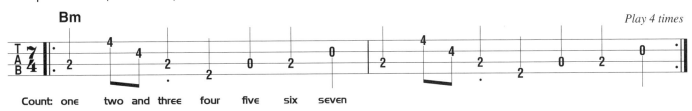

Count: one two and three four five six seven

A **6/8 time signature** means there are six beats in each measure, and an eighth note receives one beat. All note and rest values are proportionate to the eighth note. In other words, a quarter note receives two beats, a sixteenth note receives a half beat, and so on. In 6/8 time, the 1st and 4th beats are emphasized.

IRIS

"Iris" is a song by alternative rock band the Goo Goo Dolls.

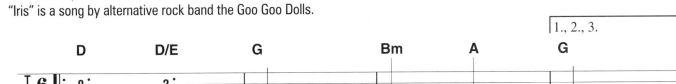

Count: one (two three) four (five six) one (two three four five six) etc.

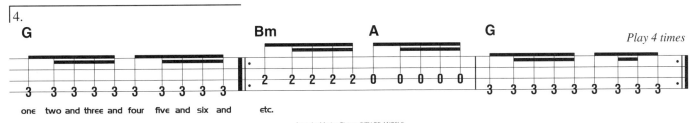

one two and three and four five and six and etc.

YOU'VE GOT TO HIDE YOUR LOVE AWAY 🔊

This song is another example of the Beatles' wonderful contribution to music. Notice the root–5th bass line on the C and D chords.

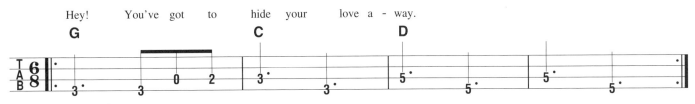

SLAP BASS

Slap bass is a popular technique for bass guitar that produces a percussive, rhythmic sound at the beginning of a note. To execute this technique, your thumb slaps against the lower strings to sound like a kick drum, and your index finger pulls on the higher strings to make a popping sound much like a snare.

Let's start with the **thumb slap**. Make a loose fist with your plucking hand and stick out your thumb like you're about to hitchhike [Photo 1]. Keep your hand in this shape and use the middle joint on your thumb to slap against the string [Photo 2]. The slap sound comes from the string hitting the metal frets where the neck meets the body of the bass. Keep your arm and wrist loose enough so that your thumb bounces back off the string after striking. This will allow the slapped note to sustain.

Photo 1

Photo 2

THUMBING 🔊

First, try to get a good slap sound with your thumb by playing slow quarter notes on the low E and A strings. When you feel a bit more confident with this new technique, try this rhythm. Use your fretting hand to dampen the string for the muted note and for rests.

YOU CAN CALL ME AL 🔊

"You Can Call Me Al" is a song by Paul Simon that features Bakithi Kumalo on bass.

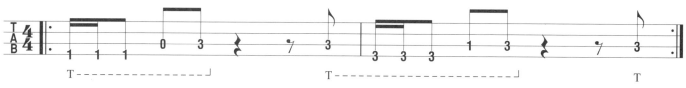

LESSONS IN LOVE 🔊

Let's speed it up a little with this song by British musical group Level 42. This is a great workout for the thumb slap!

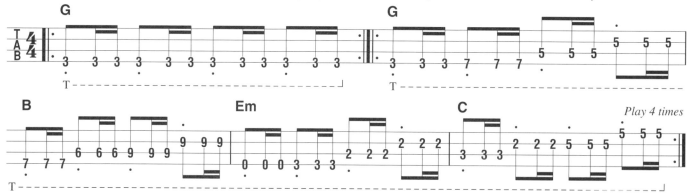

Once comfortable with the thumb slap, we can add the **finger pop**. Since the pop is an extension of the thumb slap, all you need to do is make a hook with your index finger to grab the string [Photo 3], pull up away from the fretboard [Photo 4] and release. When released, the string should snap back and hit the upper frets, creating the percussive pop sound. Use forearm movement when alternating between your thumb slapping down and your finger pulling up for the pop.

Photo 3

Photo 4

THANK YOU (FALLETINME BE MICE ELF AGAIN)

This is an R&B classic by Sly and the Family Stone. Their bass player, Larry Graham, was an early innovator of the slap style.

FLY AWAY

Earlier in this book, we played the chorus part of "Fly Away" by Lenny Kravitz. Here is the bass line for the verses. Try to combine the slap and pop as one fluid movement. This song uses a slight flange effect on the bass to get its signature, funky sound.

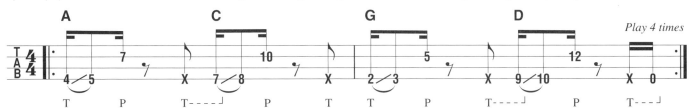

TREASURE

It's quite common for slap bass lines to include octaves, as this Bruno Mars song demonstrates. The octave shape lends itself to an alternating slap–pop motion.

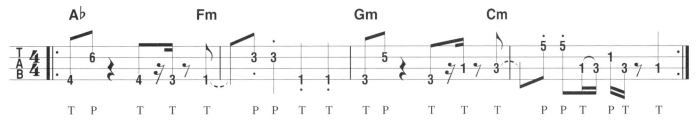

HIGHER GROUND

"Higher Ground" is a song written by Stevie Wonder in 1973. Close to 20 years later, the Red Hot Chili Peppers released a raucous cover version as the first single from their album *Mother's Milk,* featuring this great slap bass line.

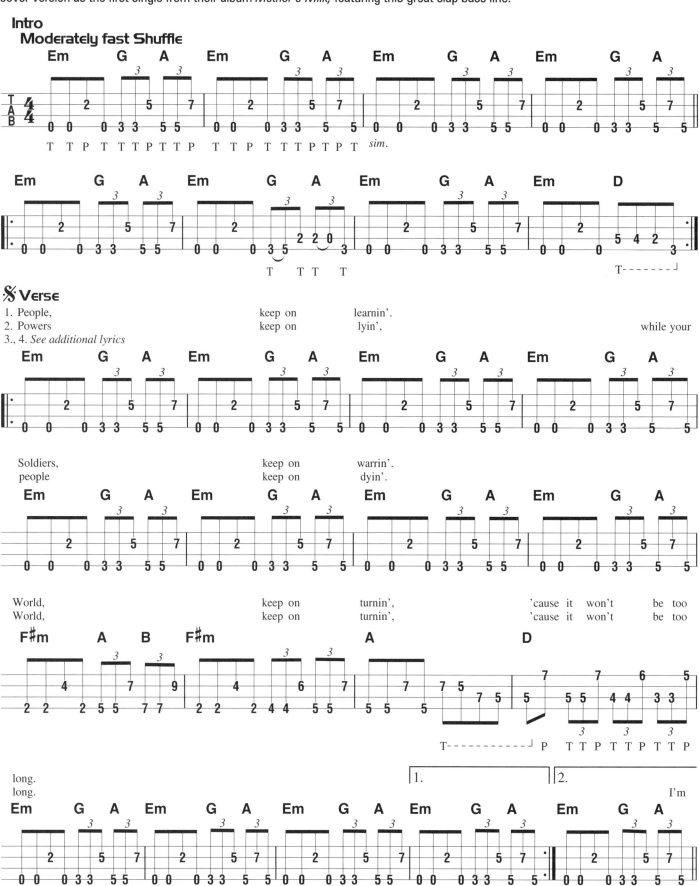

Chorus

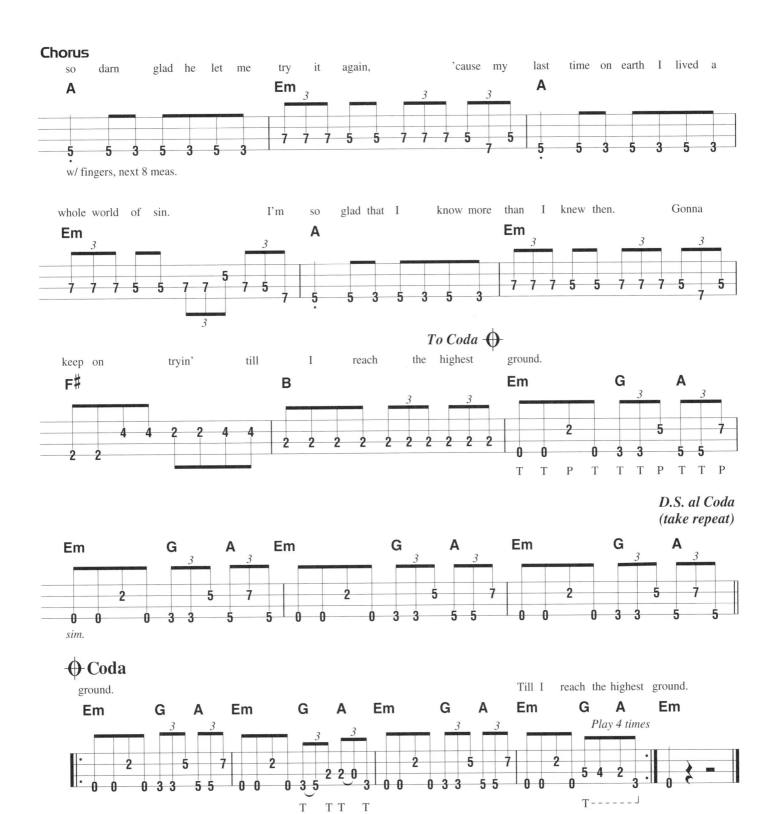

Additional Lyrics

3. Teachers, keep on teachin'.
   Preachers, keep on preachin'.
   World, keep on turnin',
   'Cause it won't be too long.

4. Lovers, keep on lovin'
   While believers keep on believin'.
   Sleepers, just stop sleepin'
   'Cause it won't be too long.

AEROPLANE

Let's finish with one more Red Hot Chili Peppers song excerpt. Flea is renowned for his great slap bass playing, and the verse section of "Aeroplane" is another superb example. In the chorus, when there's a slide down from the high G (10th fret), wait till beat 2 to begin the slide down.

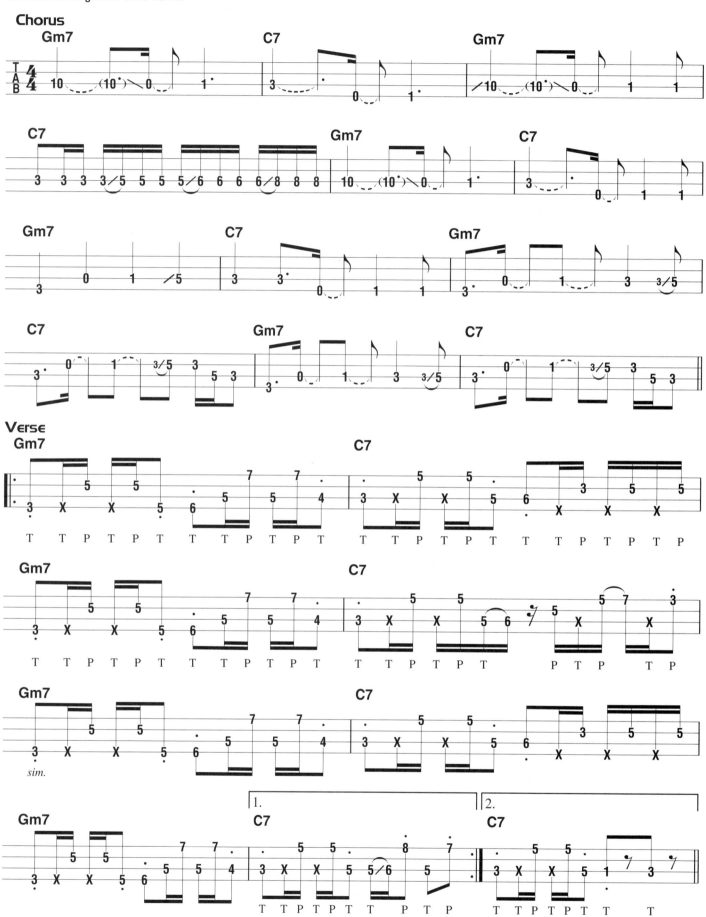